ZELDA

Frontier Life in America

a fantasy in three parts

by

KAYE McDONOUGH

City Lights Books
San Francisco

Cover: snapshot of Zelda Fitzgerald, 1920

Library of Congress Cataloging in Publication Data

McDonough, Kaye, 1943 —
   Zelda

   1. Fitzgerald, Zelda Sayre, in fiction, drama,
poetry, etc. I. Title.
PS3563.A29145Z3   812'.5'4   78-15332
ISBN: 0-87286-104-X

CITY LIGHTS BOOKS are edited by Lawrence Ferlinghetti
& Nancy J. Peters at the City Lights Bookstore, Columbus and
Broadway, San Francisco, California 94133.

This book is dedicated to
Frank Sears and Butch Leslie

AUTHOR'S PREFACE

ZELDA is Mind Theatre, a mental performance piece in which characters move brain left and brain right. As in a fantasy (*imaginative fiction featuring esp. strange settings and grotesque characters*), I indulge in unlicensed distortion. However, a host of particulars in ZELDA is accurate to the Fitzgerald's lives. The peonies Zelda ties to her waist, the ragged robins and black tulips were favorite flowers. The Alice in Wonderland lampshades, fox coat, flesh-colored bathing suit, Zelda's "indian eyes," the Garden of Allah Hotel, the swimming and diving, "the very rich are different from us," Shirley Temple/Freddy Bartholomew letter are among the factual references. The reader unfamiliar with the real-life characters in this piece may be interested to know that the biographical information in Virginia Woolf's prologue is true—other than the obvious discrepancies (Virginia Woolf never met the Fitzgeralds, was never involved in their lives and so on); Woolf's dialogue as a spectre is taken from her own suicide note (see Appendix). In fact, much dialogue spoken by all of the characters is based on actual statements. For example, readers of Hemingway's *A Moveable Feast* will recognize his statements about the Fitzgeralds.

Concerning the larger questions of character, I have freely used biographical material. The central outline—the courtship, marriage, alcoholism, Zelda's efforts to paint, write and dance, her breakdown & death by fire—follows Zelda's life. The Art Critics in Part III quote reviews of her work which appeared in *Time* (1934), and *The Baltimore Evening Sun* (1933). I have paraphrased Scott Fitzgerald: "I married the heroine of my stories." "I am the professional novelist, and I am supporting you. That is all my material. None of it is your material." "You are a third rate writer and a third rate ballet dancer." And Zelda herself: "If I had not explored my abysses in public . . ." "Suddenly last spring I began to see all red while I worked or I saw no colors . . ." "Now I am here Valmont Sanitorium . . . in a situation where I cannot be anybody, full of vertigo, with an increasing noise in my ears, feeling the vibrations of everyone I meet. Broken down." Or, more to the point of her character an inscription she wrote on a photo, "What the hell, Zelda Sayre."

By these references, I don't mean to suggest that ZELDA is a scholarly work. I have taken enormous liberties, the most flagrant of which is the dream sequence in the Province of Desire, loosely based on an incident in Zelda's life in which she, dressed as a man, accompanied Scott on a nightlife tour of Soho, and amalgamated with my own nightlife tours of North Beach, San Francisco.

To those interested in the background of Zelda's life, I recommend the classic biographies: Nancy Milford's *Zelda* (Harper & Row) and Andrew Turnbull's *Scott Fitzgerald* (Charles Scribners). Zelda's own writings, for example, *Save Me the Waltz* and *Bits of Paradise: 22 Uncollected Stories by F. Scott and Zelda Fitzgerald* (Scribners), abound in autobiographical material as do Scott Fitzgerald's, in particular, *The Beautiful and Damned*, in which he drew heavily on Zelda's diaries and letters, and *Tender is the Night*, a fictional treatment of Zelda's breakdown. Interesting photographs and color reproductions of Zelda's paintings can be found in *The Romantic Egoists*, edited by M. J. Bruccoli, Scottie Fitzgerald Smith and Joan P. Kerr (Charles Scribners).

For some other perspectives on the Fitzgeralds, try Edmund Wilson: *The Twenties*, Ernest Hemingway: *The Moveable Feast*, Anita Loos: *Kiss Hollywood Goodbye*, Aaron Latham: *Crazy Sundays*, and Calvin Tomkins, *Living Well is the Best Revenge* which contains Gerald Murphy's reminiscenses of Zelda, the most moving I have read.

I would like to add a note of thanks to Elizabeth Warner who first expressed interest in publishing ZELDA, to St. Clement's Theatre in New York which produced it, and my appreciation and love to my dear friends Neeli Cherkovski, Kaye Cofini, Bob Sharrard and Nancy Peters.

—Kaye McDonough

Self Portrait by Zelda Fitzgerald

Zelda and Scott — Montgomery 1921

The brightness of a receding flame tricks the eye
or is that crazy night vision real
that makes a driver swerve from on oncoming town?

We stare into the night sky
at stars that have died (vision is that slow)
to watch the constellations of memory rise
where all the distance between two points is pain
and even the straightest line must bend
through the past
through the past
through the most grievous past

DRAMATIS PERSONNAE

ZELDA FITZGERALD (maiden name SAYRE) is the heroine. Athletic like a swimmer. Long, lean. She is charming and intense. Everything about her must project a strange, compelling energy.

SCOTT FITZGERALD (Goofo) is the poet. He is appealing and romantic, quite able to build a castle in the air. He is Zelda's ally and male counterpart. Zelda and Scott resemble each other.

ERNEST HEMINGWAY is the adversary/provocateur. Though he is beefy and loud, he is not stupid. If anything, he is sly and has an ability to undermine.

VIRGINIA WOOLF represents the Old World artist. She appears as a thin and pale woman in her late fifties. Her hair is long and greying. She wears a tailored, two-piece woman's suit that has two large pockets to hold her stones.

GERTRUDE STEIN is the teacher, mother and oracle. Dressed in a full length robe, she remains seated on a pedestal throughout the proceedings as if she were a monumental statue. Physically she should resemble the real-life Gertrude Stein. Gertrude Stein also plays:

MADAME EGOROVA, Zelda's ballet instructor and
ZELDA'S MOTHER

VOICE, the **TYRANNY OF SMILES LEERERS** and the **ART CRITICS' VOICES** can be played by several males or they can be suggested by a single voice, depending on how many players the Director sees fit to use.

VIRGINIA WOOLF'S PROLOGUE

VIRGINIA WOOLF'S PROLOGUE

Stage is hung with chiffon or gauze-like net in sheets. Appearing through veils is Gertrude Stein on a pedestal. She keeps a seated motionless posture throughout the play, moving only her head or hands; these movements are slight and rigid.

In front of the veils is a small table that holds a cigarette case, a box of wooden matches and a photograph album.

Enter Virginia Woolf.

VIRGINIA WOOLF   Good evening, ladies and gentlemen. I am Virginia Woolf, first lady of English letters, here to introduce to you the reminiscences of the late, demented Mrs. Fitzgerald, insane wife of the late American novelist and alcoholic, Scott Fitzgerald. Three other players are featured: Mr. Hemingway, novelist and suicide, Miss Stein, novelist and enigma, and . . . me. Why me? Well may you ask. I myself don't understand but I have been chosen to play a part, and I have always agreed to play my part. I have a modest role as spectre . . . [*Virginia removes pins from her hair, which is long and greying. She shakes it loose.*] . . . hence these unsightly bulges in my pockets. [*She pats her pockets affectionately.*]

ZELDA   [*offstage throughout Virginia Woolf's Prologue. Voice only*] Tell them, Vah-gin-ya!

VIRGINIA   [*slightly irritated*] Stones, you know. Despite my fortuitous marriage to Leonard, despite my famous friendships, despite my brilliant career in *les belles lettres* . . .

ZELDA   [*bored*] Yes, yes.

VIRGINIA   [*trying to keep her dignity*] . . . I suffered a debilitating, recurring madness . . .

15

ZELDA   Tell them, Vah-gin-ya.

VIRGINIA   . . . you might call it a . . .

ZELDA   Yes?

VIRGINIA   . . . a—how would one say? —death of the spirit.
I drowned myself in the River Ouse near our home in Rod-
mell by weighting my pockets with stones . . . *these* stones.
[*Virginia Woolf, in an aside, shows them to the audience.
The stones are ovals of smooth white marble*] Beautiful,
aren't they? I'd hate to give them up! . . . Modern technology has opened up so many avenues of suicide to us
since then: appliances, ovens and the like . . . why automobiles alone! the possibilities! Think of it! But I still pre-
fer the Old World way. Drowning does have its charm and
certainly produces the desired effect . . . cessation of
breath. . . In any event, now I am dead . . .

ZELDA   You can say that again!

VIRGINIA   [*beginning to lose her composure speaking more
loudly*] . . . and Mrs. Fitzgerald is, too, whether she knows
it or not! [*nearly shouting*] For her it's OVER!

ZELDA   Never over.

VIRGINIA   [*to Zelda*] Will you please be quiet . . .

ZELDA   None of it is ever over.

VIRGINIA   . . . and let me finish this prologue in peace?

ZELDA   All right, Virginia, but I'll be back.

VIRGINIA   [*looks to the side to make sure Zelda is gone*]
There! Disturbing woman! Now then . . . where was I? [*she
thinks a moment, then brightens*] Oh, yes! *We are dead!*
[*she smiles*]

GERTRUDE STEIN   F - A - C - T

Virginia does not hear Gertrude Stein's voice. She wanders to the table and chair, takes a cigarette holder from one of her pockets, takes a cigarette from case on the table, places it in her holder and lights. She sits down. Throughout the following monologue she smokes, opens and closes photograph album, sometimes holds up album to show audience, sometimes looks through it on the table.

VIRGINIA   Zelda . . . *[aside]* God! Only an American could have such a name! . . . was born at the outset of the twentieth century (that's right, in 1900) to a prominent and respected Southern family *[aside]* (total provincials) . . . the Sayres. They were odd, but not too odd! Her mother [*Virginia flips through book, finds photo, holds album up and points to photo]* was Minnie Machen, "The Wild Lily of the Cumberland," *[sets album down]* who wrote poetry and wanted to go on the stage. Her family objected and she ended up marrying [*Virginia picks up album again, shows audience]* . . . him . . . *[reads caption]* "Anthony Dickenson Sayre, elected to the Alabama State Senate, elected Judge of the City Court, Montgomery, Alabama." [*Virginia sets book down]* He was reserved.

They had six children, the youngest of whom was Zelda. Here she is again in costume . . . no date, but she's older all right.

Here's an even later photo of Mrs. Fitzgerald with her mother . . . and who is that man on the right? [*Virginia studies photo]* God! It's Scott Fitzgerald . . . let me see . . . 1938, 39, 40 . . . yes . . . three years before he died in Hollywood. Look at that expression: ruin, debauchery, fear . . . The Last Tycoon indeed . . . and look here [*Virginia puts face close to photo to study it]* . . . the lettering on the window behind Zelda and her mother . . . What is that?

Zelda's Mother, Zelda, Scott, 1938

[*reads*] "N D H O" . . . must be Highland Hospital for the Insane in Asheville, North Carolina . . . Zelda was in and out of there the last 15 years of her life. [*Confidentially*] Oh, yes, her marriage to Mr. Fitzgerald wasn't quite the golden idyll . . . Zelda went totally mad . . . they said . . . That's what they said. After all the high old times in New York and Paris, she was sent back to the South and died in a fire at this hospital on March 10, 1948. [*Virginia closes album and reflects. She re-opens it, flips through it again*] . . . Though I had the good fortune to avoid knowing the Fitzgeralds (they were part of that sideshow known as Paris in the Twenties) and considered them to be silly people, I can't leave them there.

[*Virginia finds another photo*] Here's one of Zelda, in her white fox coat, with Scott in the lobby of the Biltmore Hotel, "New York, 1921": Mr. and Mrs. Jazz Age. Here they are on the Boulevard St. Michel with Scottie, their little girl, "Paris, 1924": Mr. and Mrs. Expatriate. Here's a lovely one: Scott and Scottie and Zelda on the Beach at Antibes: Mr. and Mrs. Happily-Ever-After. I must admit, they were beautiful . . . and here . . . [*Virginia stops in horror*] Oh Lord! What is this? Zelda at the Gorge of Constantine, 1930 . . . She's only 30 . . . bent over . . . and that face . . . [*Virginia slams book shut, lays her head in her arm on top of the album, then composes herself*] I can't look any more.

Who were these people, anyway, and why am I upset? Why dredge them up again? What did they have to do with anything important!

GERTRUDE STEIN   Spirit beyond gender.

Virginia picks up a piece of paper that has fallen from the photo album

VIRGINIA   Now what is this?

GERTRUDE STEIN   F - A - C - T

VIRGINIA   [*Not hearing Gertrude Stein, she reads:*]
   "*The pure products of America go crazy—... .*"
   [*Virginia looks up from paper*] What about me? Wasn't *I*
   effective? [*reads:*]
         "*It is only in isolate flecks that*
         something
         is given off

         No one
         to witness
         and adjust,
                  no one to drive the car"

What is that supposed to mean? Really! Other than Tom
Eliot's, most American poetry leave me cold! Who wrote
this? [*reads:*] "William Carlos Williams, New Jersey" *(Virginia looks up*] New Jersey? I ask you! The mind reels! [*She
replaces paper in the album*] That is all *I* have to say, We'd
best get on with this. Begin!

         Virginia Woolf exits

ZELDA'S PROLOGUE

ZELDA'S PROLOGUE

Same stage set with Gertrude Stein behind veils. Enter Zelda wearing white leotard wraparound dress. She is radiant.

ZELDA   Some welcome Virginia gave you! I hope she didn't put you off! Oh dear people, I wouldn't want to put you through a difficult time . . . though you know sometimes life is . . . well . . . let's put it this way . . . not easy. You know that.

Gladly I'd tidy up my life and make a smile of it. I could wear the disguise of "Oh, Yes, that's fine" and "Please some more." I could say in a voice to convince you, "Oh yes. Today as always everything is OK." But what can be done with fact and what done with feeling? You'd recognize the lie. So I'll try to be true. You are alive and in the living state. You know what it is. How could I fool you? Why would I want to?

I stretch out my arms to you! [*Zelda opens her arms and walks forward*] Come in! Please! Take what you want! Welcome! [*Zelda bumps into table*] What's this? [*Sees album, flips through*] So that's what Virginia was looking at. Now look at this! [*She stares at photo in disbelief and shows audience*] Were we ever those unalterable beings? Here's another! [*Holds up album*] Oh, Scott . . . [*her tone changes as she addresses Scott (offstage) she talks to him almost as if she were talking to herself*] Our lives together are as distant as photographs of a war. I've looked for us in the pictures. Who were we? Halted frames in an onrush of being. What were we becoming? [*Zelda holds up another photo, sets it down and mimics a photographer*] The dispassionate eye recedes, a turn, adjusts the f-stop, click . . . Locks heat!

I see us, images, there. [Freeze!] I look at my life as if it were maybe someone else's. [*Looks at more photos*]

Wretched beings trapped in a past or parallel or future! Let the life of us sear through! The alive beings we were! A fit, a flash, a blaze of being! Heat, warp the frame!

[*Zelda stands on her head and says:*] Now! Blood courses through my body. If you could feel it as I do. Pulse knocking at my ears, valve constriction, blood rush and pump! [*Zelda rights herself and looks at where she was*] Listen! . . . The lyric stands on its head! Inverted!

Let the song of my life pour out, let it surge, til the averted eye come head on in, til the stone stare swim! Let all the metal measures molten be! [*She takes a match from the table*] Heat! [*Strikes it*] Warp! [*Puts flame to photo*] Oh! There it goes again! [*Burns photo*] Enough of the straight jacket! I throw open the barred windows of my life to you! Souls, everywhere, you know what it is to be alive! Welcome!

Curtain closes on Zelda

PART I

PART I

Same stage arrangement with veils. The table is gone. Gertrude Stein is still seated behind veils. Scott, who is dressed in a WWI army uniform, stands stage left behind veil. Ernest, in huntsmen's clothes and carrying gun, stands further back in darkened area of stage. He is barely visible. Stage right, in front of veils, is a ladder leading to a diving platform. Below the platform is a rectangular area marked by molding. It is painted aqua and has a light inside it, representing a chlorine swimming pool. Zelda enters wearing the same white dancer's dress. She climbs the ladder and stands on the parapet. With one quick motion, she removes her dress, revealing a flesh-colored bathing suit. She takes a diver's position at the edge of the platform and calls out:

ZELDA   The air shines and it is yellow and white at the same time! This is the gift air and the day holding round it! I want (I wanted) to blow into life a brilliance as into a flame to fan it! I want (I wanted) *you* know, *everything!*

SCOTT   [*who has come forward to observe her*] Who is the golden window opening on air? Who is she there? [*he points at her*]

VOICE   [*offstage*] Don't you know? That is Zelda Sayre.

SCOTT   Alarming beauty on the brink of all of it, ready to plummet. No fear in her. Nothing but light.

Zelda throws arms back making ready to dive

ZELDA   I am not destroyed by gravity!

VOICE   [*offstage*] Zelda! Stop!

27

ZELDA   Never pull back! (Shit! Who would ask it?) I dive!

Lights darken to suggest her dive. Sound of object entering water. Silence. Long pause. Lights come up again. Zelda rises from a crouched position as if leaving a body of water. While Scott speaks, she puts on her dress again.

SCOTT   [*to audience*] She rose up with finest silt in her hair from the river bed. She'd hit the deepest mark.

VOICE   [*offstage*] Zelda, what is it?

ZELDA   [*to audience*] Weird. I knew it then and should have held to it but didn't. I should have kept that rock and added others. I did not. I should have. I would dive again . . . but I hated to tell them what I saw there . . . It would spoil their afternoon. I hated to tell them . . . there . . . sliding around me as a net was hair, the hair of her, Virginia, even then, and placed in my hand this remembrance . . . a stone, a weight I could not handle [*Zelda shows in her hand a marble stone resembling Virginia's*]

ERNEST   She'll ruin you, Scott.

SCOTT   And weighting her hand a large white stone. She had the queerest look . . . her eyes dead level and unafraid. She threw the stone back in the water [*Zelda tosses stone away as he says this*] saying: "I can swim with weights . . ."

ZELDA   [*overlapping Scott*] I can swim with weights . . .

SCOTT   ". . . but I swim better without."

ZELDA   . . . but I swim better without.

28

ERNEST   I knew the first time I saw her she was crazy.

SCOTT   So easily she cast it off . . . No bump . . . not a single
bruise. She went in so clean . . . Her body came up perfectly
and her perfectly level look. I loved her.

ZELDA   I had hit the water hard FWACK How else from so
great a height and once below I was entrappéd by hair and
the spectre there. The weight of water pushed my lungs.
The hair ensnarled me. The water pressed and pressed and
held me there. Virginia pressed the stone pushing me
down. Bitch. I might have drowned . . . might have but did
not. I surfaced. I had broken three small bones in my left
hand. [*Scott takes her hand and kisses it*] Scott kissed it,
not knowing.

*Scott bows to Zelda and exits. Ernest disappears. Sound of
water lapping. Virginia, as spectre, enters. Her hair is loose.
She is hunched over from the stones in her pockets. She roams
around behind the veils unaware of anything being said to her.
The stage is darkened as if it were evening.*

ZELDA   Oh Vah-*gin*-ya!

VIRGINIA   [*in trance-like chant:*] We had a good life. We
were as happy as two people could possibly be.

ZELDA   Vah-*gin*-ya!

VIRGINIA   [*unable to hear*] It wasn't our life was *un*happy.
No. Just that I — I — couldn't — again . . .

ZELDA   Virginia. You at it *again*, honey? What are you trying to do to yourself dragging around with those stones in
your pockets?

VIRGINIA   I couldn't go through it again. We had a good life. We were as happy as two people could possibly be.

GERTRUDE STEIN   [*motionless except for barely perceptible hand and head gestures*] Look at her look at her look at her then them silly woman silly girl. Moo moo towns and udder nonsense silly. Majestic she said of herself being who she was then look look look.

Zelda looks. Virginia moves offstage. Zelda calls after her:

ZELDA   For chrissake, Virginia, take those stones out of your pockets. You're going to *drown* out there. Do you hear me? *Drown!*

VIRGINIA   We were happy . . .

Virginia exits. Zelda exits shortly afterwards.

GERTRUDE STEIN   Decoy I am. I present a strange puzzle. The unyielding woman puzzle of sexuality it is the puzzle who I am. Who am I? To be dealt with to be not. Made of rock I am who am I rock, a weight, a weighty puzzle. Man or woman. Woman man. Gender recedes before feeling and feeling a weight, a weight in the hand, a piece of a puzzle.

Enter Ernest, same costume, carrying gun, with Scott, still in WWI outfit. They are drunk and laughing. Their arms are around each other's shoulders. When Ernest spots Gertrude Stein he begins to throw pebbles at her. He and Scott are singing:

*Scott & Ernest
Meet the Sibyl*

SCOTT AND ERNEST—[*to the tune of Here We Go Round the Mulberry Bush*] "Here we go round the prick-e-ley bush, the prick-e-ley bush. Here we go round the prick-e-ley bush, so early in the evening." Ha ha ha ha ha haha.

SCOTT [*becoming composed and gentlemanly addresses statue*] Miss Stein, are you Pallas Athene, goddess of wisdom, there? Oracle? Who?

GERTRUDE STEIN They must test me.

ERNEST [*shoots at statue followed by sound effect "ping."
Fires again. Veil tears. A chip flies off the statue*] That's the only chip off the block that old dike's ever going to see . . . har har har har har [*pause*] . . . I inserted my throbbing manhood into the valley of her undoing, but the neighboring hills were rock then gravel . . . old gravel ass . . . har har har har [*to Scott:*] They're there for the taking, old man, as long as you aren't scared of getting your *you-know* broken off. Of course, with an organ of *my* size and strength, I don't have to worry about *that!* I *told* you. Go to the Louvre to the Classical models . . . the statues there . . . See how *I* stack up against the Greeks.

GERTRUDE STEIN Geometry of feeling.

SCOTT You have an odd approach to passion, friend.

Ernest shoots at statue. The sound of "ping" is now a full rifle "blast."

ERNEST It's rock and poke and that's the way it's played.

31

SCOTT [*aside*] As if we were chunks of marble subject to mathematical rules.

ERNEST [*blast*] Angles of entry!

GERTRUDE STEIN Theorems.

ERNEST [*shoots—blast*] Oh I know how to proposition, all right! Is that what you mean? Ha ha. [*gestures to Gertrude*] You can forget *this* one. You'll never lay her.

SCOTT [*studies statue of Gertrude Stein*] I think you make her seem too hard.

GERTRUDE STEIN [*gesturing to Ernest*] This one thinks he has to deal with me but does not know who I am.

ERNEST Miss Stein.

GERTRUDE STEIN No.

SCOTT She is not an unfeeling creature.

GERTRUDE STEIN I am another form of feeling. [*in a chant*] I never kisséd, I never kisséd, I never kisséd anyone's ass except Alice's.[*to audience, referrring to Ernest*] His order violates feeling.

SCOTT [*on one knee to Gertrude Stein*] Plait me a garland even if it be graven, grave, grave, graven Gertrude, O stone lady, thou who art raiséd from the river bed wherein one weights herself with stones. Let a tiny fissure of passion through, maybe through minute cavities of air among tiniest ground stones, concrete ground rock and sand. O most unyielding lady, neither break apart, nor split, nor crack before me, only yield. I bend and bend before you wanting to take you in.

GERTRUDE STEIN   [*referring to Scott*] This one's a different case: poet. He sees me he sees me truly and looks for a way into it, that is the block, the rock of feeling. [*to Scott:*] I would change then change I would even to sand, not for man, not for gender of it. I say geography of feeling does not find itself in an organ. No. [*referring to Scott*] This one's map's my own. No moo quack of gender here. Not a socket I, no, I not a socket to be plugged, no appliance the death of me, still allow for me . . .

ERNEST   [*begins now the first of a series of commands to an offstage skeet blind. From here on out, when he calls, "Pull," a clay pigeon flies across the back of the stage, he fires at it, the audience hears the noise of a gun (indicated by "[blast]" in the dialogue) followed by the sound of the clay target shattering. The gun and skeet may be imaginary as long as representative noises are made that correspond to* Pull *and* blast *in the dialogue.*]

GERTRUDE STEIN   Allow for me . . .[*blast*]

ERNEST: Pull!

GERTRUDE STEIN   Childless . . .[*blast*]

ERNEST   Pull!

GERTRUDE STEIN   Unbreakable . . .[*blast*]

ERNEST   Pull!

GERTRUDE STEIN   Each perfection knows its flaw. [*blast*]

Zelda enters, but Scott and Ernest don't see her. She moves toward Scott

GERTRUDE STEIN [*able to see Zelda. Refers to Zelda and Scott:*] These two one artist make. I see their sweet drawing together.

ZELDA [*unheard by Scott and Ernest*] I want . . .

SCOTT I want . . .

GERTRUDE STEIN Nobody will have, not have all of it, not surely, though they want . . .

SCOTT I wanted . . .

ZELDA I wanted . . .

GERTRUDE STEIN This is the puzzle perfection puzzle piece will not certainly be whole. Sexuality a piece of the puzzle, a piece of the puzzle only.

Ernest exits. The lights dim. Stage is dark except one light shines from the area that suggests the swimming pool. Scott lies down by it, props himself on one elbow and dips his hand in the water now and then. Zelda walks forward to address audience.

ZELDA Scott and I had a lovely dream . . . there at the beginning in the heat of summer by water running. Did I know then what our dream was? I think I recognized it.

SCOTT [*from a distance*] We only wanted wonder without end!

ZELDA O chlorine stupor!

*Scott & Zelda
at the Chlorine
Pool:
The Dangers of
Clear Water*

SCOTT   What was the matter with *that*?

ZELDA   Aqua oblivion . . . Then is now again.

Zelda takes her place next to Scott by the pool. He loosens his jacket then takes it off. From time to time Zelda runs her hand through the water.

SCOTT   [*to Zelda*] Dearest, we'll always have our aqua pool . . . though we be poor as peasants . . . well, not *that* poor. I'll give you a diamond as big as the Ritz. We'll have an estate and a soda shop. We'll pledge ourselves to one another forever and be free. We'll be expatriates and real Americans. We'll know everything and be innocent. We'll be famous and simple, transient and permanent, beautiful and plain. No prophylactics in our doorway! We'll have a great past . . . an endless future and no one will have to work or suffer again! We'll have everything and it will happen all at the same time! Won't it be wonderful? I can hardly wait for it to start!

ZELDA   [*to audience*] I was never a naive child . . . not then . . . not now . . . but I couldn't quite face what he was saying . . .

GERTRUDE STEIN   They bought the wrong dream.

ZELDA   I couldn't quite face . . .

GERTRUDE STEIN   Couldn't and didn't want to.

ZELDA   Our aqua pool was enabled by greed.

GERTRUDE STEIN   They bought the wrong dream.

ZELDA   All wrong.

GERTRUDE STEIN It was easily bought, they thought.

ZELDA The wrong dream.

SCOTT [*transported—looking into the distance*] How the heat waves up from the sand's beige bands . . . blue water . . . blue sky and clean white sails! O those neat triangles waving a bit but right-angled all the same, still identifiable for all the stress of motion . . .

GERTRUDE STEIN [*spells*] F - A - C - T

SCOTT [*Unhearing to Zelda*] . . . band on band of shore, sea, sky. I see you, dear, rising like a land mass after a long sea voyage, obscured by dazzling heat . . . continent, illimitable and vast whose shores erode even as I approach . . . embrace of sand.

ZELDA [*to audience*] "Embrace of sand" He had something there.

SCOTT Inexhaustible frontier!

ZELDA [*still to audience*] And the truth of it was I was an ordinary girl and had my limits. Isn't that the way with it? In the greenhouses we cultivate another country's weeds. [*to Scott who doesn't seem to hear:*] Oh, Goofo, to see you there, so stricken by hope and promise. I wish I hadn't seen it for what it was . . . all consuming greed . . . you made it sound so nice! [*Zelda thinks about this for a moment and plays with the water*] The water seems clear [*pause, she plays some more*] . . . and contained. But . . . [*Zelda gasps*]

SCOTT [*hears her*] What is it?

ZELDA There, do you see? I'd almost forgotten about her. O Scott. How long do you think she's been down there? [*to spectre in pool*] Vah-gin-ya! Virginia. [*to Scott*] Look at

36

her, Scott! She's wrinkled and cords of grey hair stream from her head. She's too old to be Ophelia. God! She slides like a snake!

Voice of VIRGINIA WOOLF [*chants*] I feel certain I am going mad again. I don't think two people could have been happier than we have been. We were as happy as two people could possibly be.

ZELDA [*to audience*] This was the first Scott had seen her. I shouted to her [*Zelda shouts*] "Virginia, get out of there. Get out of our pool!" but it didn't do any good.

SCOTT Zelda wasn't afraid of anything.

ZELDA If you want to know, I was disgusted. What did she want anyway? She had teacakes on a tray and surely all the watercress one woman could stand. [*Zelda calls out!*] "Vah-gin-ya, come up on out of there, girl!" I couldn't stand to see her there, old and sinking further to a bottom.

"Scott!" (I called to him wrongly, he could not purge her) "Get rid of her, Goofo!" [*She shakes Scott—He takes notice*] For all his poet's blood and silver hope I knew he could not reach the drowned dream of her. Nobody touches the deepest level of need . . . yet Scott tried. I loved him for trying.

SCOTT [*standing up*] Virginia Woolf, spectre of ennui and the *belles letters* death, aristocrat *engloutie*, swimming there in the clearest of clear water, in water that is shining and pure and full of night light, Slide away, O Snake, from Eden. Agéd Ophelia, who was not even saved by love, what was it you wanted that now you haunt the lovers? [*Scott has arm of flowers he's picked by the pool. He drops them in the water as he speaks*] Rain on you dandelions and marigolds and send you on your weedy, stinking way. [*he tosses flowers*] Disappear! [*aside, in horror:*] (Look! She changes

37

shape and is an old man, too. Good Lord, does Zelda see the figure there? Sexless despair . . . I see a narcissism in her transformation . . . the convenience of androgyny . . . There, the creature beyond hope or need, not existing in the realm of desire.)

GERTRUDE STEIN   Success won't save you.

SCOTT   [*to Zelda*] There's nothing to be worried about, Zelda. [*aside*] (like hell). [*to Zelda*] Everything's going to be OK. [*aside*] if you can stand it. [*to Zelda*] I love you. [*aside*] whatever *that* is. [*to Zelda*] and Virginia's going to come out of our pool if I have to go down there and pull her up!

GERTRUDE STEIN   Passion will not touch her ruined hope.

ZELDA   [*to audience*] But Virginia had disappeared and I knew Scott was lying.

SCOTT   [*head in hands*] We only wanted everything.

ZELDA   Perhaps we were bound to be disappointed.

Sound of gun blast. Enter Ernest with his gun

ERNEST   No time for rare and expensive brains when it's guts ball, bub. [*he yells:*] Pull! [*Clay pigeon flies up. He fires. Blast*] The individual sets off in this world. There's an unending spectrum at his disposal. Isn't this what America's all about? The Last Great Experiment of Western Civilization. Pull! The Arena of Wonder! [*blast*] The Unending Dream! . . . Pull! . . . The Self! [*blast*] . . . *Pull!* . . . and Action! [*blast*]

GERTRUDE STEIN   They bought the wrong dream. It was easily bought, they thought. They bought the dream and it was not for sale.

ERNEST [*continuing*] I'm going to tell you jello heads a
thing or two. [*Ernest looks around*] Has that old bag gone?
OK. The individual sets himself a target, see? [*Ernest
takes sight with his gun*] He aims for it, see? Like this,
see? and whether there's a straight line in the universe or
not, he makes one, see? The straight line to the target. Pull!
[*blast*] There's only one thing wrong. The trajectory of the
bullet is slightly curved. It is not perfectly straight. But
the linear mind can overcome this by hitting the target before its apogee. This is the secret of linear velocity.

> I want to do away with arcs!
> The bullet is slowed by friction, mass in air.
> I long for the vacuum!
> Pull!
> The frictionless shot [*blast*]   *Ernest Takes on*
> Pull!   *Existence with*
> The air is too rich [*blast*]   *a Rational Mind*
> Pull!

ZELDA You tear it invisibly.

ERNEST Blow out the drag of feeling. Blast away the elipse
[*blast*] Pull, Pull!

Sound of yelping dog "Ai yi yi yi" on second blast

ZELDA And I thought there was nothing left to kill.

ERNEST There's always something left to kill! Pull! Linearity!
[*blast*] Action!

Curtain. End Part I

39

PART II

PART II

Same stage arrangement. Gertrude Stein on pedestal. Table and two chairs. A book, teapot, two cups, four sets of glasses (cocktail, liqueur, tall, short). On a tray are bottles of good gin, tonic, campari, cognac, a cocktail shaker and a lemon. Zelda wears a red dress (just like the white one) with a bunch of peonies at her waist. Scott, wearing a white suit and tie much like the real F. Scott Fitzgerald would have worn in the Twenties, enters as she says her opening lines. When he reaches her, she takes his arm. NOTE: Dialogue is meant to overlap, counterpoint and parallel, and move at a rapid pace.

ZELDA Scott and I married. The neat names they have for the greatest confusions.

GERTRUDE STEIN Simple names, F - A - C - T.

ZELDA Heat and confusions. All the brides lined up against a half century of laundry . . . shirts and scummy water.

SCOTT I should never have . . .

Zelda & Scott in the Province of Desire: The Marriage

ZELDA I should never have . . .

SCOTT We should never have . . .

ZELDA We should never have . . .

SCOTT Never have . . .

ZELDA Never have . . .

SCOTT Never have . . .

ZELDA Never have . . .

SCOTT   Never have . . .

ZELDA   Never have . . .

SCOTT and ZELDA   Married.

ZELDA   But Oh!

SCOTT   Oh!

ZELDA   Oh!

SCOTT   Oh!

ZELDA   He was . . .

SCOTT   She was . . .

SCOTT and ZELDA   Beautiful!

SCOTT   I should have told her . . .

ZELDA   I should have told him . . .

SCOTT   . . . her presence was enough . . .

ZELDA   . . . his presence was enough . . .

SCOTT   I should have told her . . .

ZELDA   I should have told him . . .

SCOTT   . . . she didn't have to prove anything to me or anybody else . . .

ZELDA   I should have told him . . .

SCOTT   . . . but I didn't believe it myself . . .

ZELDA   . . . it was enough for him to be . . .

SCOTT   . . . it was enough for her to be . . .

ZELDA   . . . just who he was.

SCOTT   . . . just who she was.

ZELDA   He was . . .

SCOTT   She was . . .

SCOTT and ZELDA   Beautiful!

Zelda recedes for a moment. Scott steps forward and says:

SCOTT   In all my books, I never captured her. She had an unusual way of expressing herself.

ZELDA   [*advances slowly from rear stage as she speaks. A light is on her. Her speech is rapid*] Ellipses not circles of motion unimpeded by gravity (downward pulling it pulls) I defy the spinning together of molecules on an axis instead you feel a force field peculiar to my body, the energy of this unique arrangement, compression of movement, I speak for each particle: not a perfect ball and neither moving in a circle nor a past but elliptical and perhaps contrary to the normal perceived centers of motion named gravity, gravity being only the densest part of velocity.

*Zelda Expounds
on the Nature of
the Extraordinary*

SCOTT   Sometimes she took a little explaining to people . . .

ZELDA [*rapidly*] Here in one galaxy, planets and moons boomerang around ungrounded sun. [*Zelda sighs*] Their names, their names . . . Even the *sun*, a center of *what*? Motion. And where in universes spinning into shrinking infinity? They say "rising" and "setting." Yes, yes. This up, this down. "Aye" "Aye" nods the democracy of perception.

SCOTT . . . but we had an awfully good time together.

ZELDA Mornings, high tides — that kind of relentless regularity is taken to be unalterable. They name their names. The law of this and the law of that demand a regularity unseen universes may not obey this tyranny of sense and matter. When worlds might wheel in the sky and what is predictable and downward moving might suddenly surprise and invert!

SCOTT She was a real *live wire*!

ZELDA [*very excited*] Look! Out there! Beyond the confines of this perceived space: elliptical wheel of the earth's rut is cut suddenly by a piece of matter gone berserk. It flies through space cutting proscribed ellipses of motion! Random arc of a meteor from where we sit, wouldn't the democracy of perception agree? it is, Oh Yes, yes, at approximately 2,000 feet altitude, flying out of whack, wouldn't you say? at approximately 6,000 to 8,000 miles per hour. And here we are minus our instruments. Red flashes, greenish copper blaze finishing in green (that is what we name this wave length, is it not?). Mass observes mass, mass perceives itself and its flying apart! There. Meteor. We make a name for it and a rule for its trajectory! I objectory!

SCOTT I see her now, full sailed and smiling.

ZELDA [*with happy intensity*] The air holds promise and is alive with it. Each moment is new and new ground and is not linear but touches every other moment and every other space. The energy of a life moves out, not trapped in a past, and affects every other.

Scott loves Zelda

SCOTT   I loved to look at her and hear her talk.

ZELDA   Goofo. [*Zelda walks up to Scott and holds his face in her hands with affection*]

SCOTT   I loved her [*He puts his hands on her arms*]

ZELDA   Dear.

SCOTT   Zelda on the last piece of unlegislated ground. Insane by every measure.

Zelda loves Scott

ZELDA   I loved to touch him and watch him move.

As Zelda continues this speech, Scott goes to table, sits in a chair, crosses his legs, takes a book from the table, opens it, reads, pours tea in a cup for himself and one for imaginary partner, gets up and stands against a veil. These actions synchronize with Zelda's speech. Zelda watches him but he doesn't seem to see.

ZELDA   It's hard to say what Goofo and I were to each other and why I felt close to him as to no other person in the world.

Maybe it was something ordinary he did. (I liked the way he sat in a chair.) He crossed his legs just right. (I liked the way he did that.)

I think it was something simple he did. I saw him doing it: open a book. (I liked the way he opened a book.)

Was it the cup of tea he poured or was it a stare in a shaded room? Was it the way he looked at five? —or was it 1:07 on

47

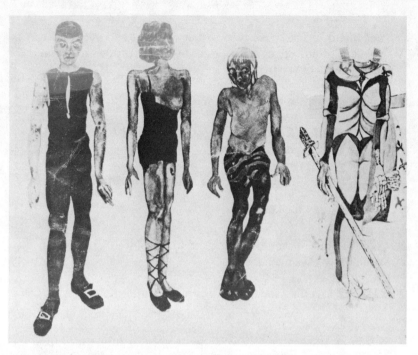

Costumes for a Children's Theatre by Zelda Fitzgerald

Antibes, 1926

May 3rd?—by the wall he stood, sunflooded and white-suited. I liked looking at him there.

Yes, some ordinary thing he did that made me know the rest was done from an excess of spirit.

He who was King of the Roses, Poet, brushed his teeth. (I loved the way he brushed his teeth.) I liked to watch him do that.

(I liked to touch him and watch him move.)

I loved him.

SCOTT   I loved her.

ZELDA   O Goofo! All you've invented and all you are! [*pause*] The open arch of your foot, I touch with the inside arch of my foot and touch along inside of my hand unsettling the hairs in the nest of your back! Wrap arms around me, Goofo, shake out the refrigerators and waffle irons! Shake out the lamps and aluminum ranges! Shake out the steam irons and console radios! Shake them out, out! And marry me all the way down!

A fuck is what they call it? Well! All *right*! Let's call it *that!* Goofo, love, I would be fucked and fucked and fucked and fuck you, love, fuck you! [*Zelda bursts out laughing*] Not everyone knows how to say *that* right! [*Then she sighs. Her face grows puzzled. She begins to pace.*] What was it all supposed to be anyhow? A tidy house?

GERTRUDE STEIN   Tidy.

ZELDA   Tidy children?

GERTRUDE STEIN   Clean.

ZELDA   Tidy afternoons on neat green lawns?

SCOTT   [*coming forward*] What went wrong?

*Zelda & Scott
Fall from
Domestic Grace*

ZELDA   I couldn't say. We set up housekeeping in Westport. One quiet evening, two quiet evenings. I lay down in front of a train for something to do.

SCOTT   Ecstasy . . . There's no holding on to it.

ZELDA   What was it we wanted?

SCOTT   What was it we wanted?

ZELDA   I'd like to say it was the desire for children . . .

SCOTT   It wasn't.

ZELDA   . . . but it wasn't.

SCOTT   We had one . . .

ZELDA   . . . a daughter . . .

SCOTT   . . . and named her Scottie, after me.

ZELDA   . . . but what we were wanting didn't come in a baby buggy . . . though I loved our girl.

SCOTT   We tried.

ZELDA   She was a little angel and her separate mortality moved me.

SCOTT   Zelda made a dollhouse and papered the miniature rooms. She painted Tweedledeedee and Tweedledeedum on Alice in Wonderland lampshades.

ZELDA   I got Scottie a nanny.

SCOTT   She got me a cook.

ZELDA   But as an earth mother I was a bust. Scott did what
he could to make up for me, but he wasn't much better.

Oh, Scottie, dear, I'm sorry [*Zelda lays her head in the
crook of her arm*]

GERTRUDE STEIN   Too far, too far
She was going too far . . .

ZELDA   I failed.

SCOTT   No one knew what too far was until somebody went.
We had one child . . .

ZELDA   That wasn't what I wanted.

SCOTT   . . . and never had another.

ZELDA   Scott didn't want any more, any more than I did.

GERTRUDE STEIN   Drivespring of the spirit
in a man's breast
in a woman's breast

ZELDA   I should never have tried to be a woman.

GERTRUDE STEIN   She tried.

ZELDA   I tried . . .

GERTRUDE STEIN   She tried and tried.

ZELDA   . . . and tried.

GERTRUDE STEIN   It was trying and did not fit.

ZELDA   I was not fit.

SCOTT   Though we fit . . .

ZELDA   We fit.

SCOTT   . . . and everything worked.

ZELDA   I tried to be a woman . . .

SCOTT   She was a woman . . .

ZELDA   They called me one . . . but I was not fit.

GERTRUDE STEIN   Woman, woman's not the key
They bray of sexuality

ZELDA   I tried.

SCOTT   She tried.

GERTRUDE STEIN   She tried and tried and tried. The size
of the try did not fit the trying.

ZELDA   I split.

SCOTT   The marriage wasn't quite what we'd wanted.

ZELDA   That's for sure! I took the liberty of investigating
other possibilities.

A group of men — —anywhere from one to five — —begin to assemble behind the veils. They stand apart in belligerent attitudes. Visible in their pockets are porno mags, dildoes, pills, and hypodermic needles. They are the TYRANNY OF SMILES LEERERS and the dialogue marked VOICE is divided among them.

ZELDA   At first, I think I could have fallen into any loving
eye. Each person has his particular gravity and I liked to

52

find it and be drawn in. But Goofo! One man took my hands and fondled them and told me I had beautiful wrists. Another sought my eye on the street. Another called out to me—

VOICE   SMILE!

ZELDA   That's an order, Goofo . . .

VOICE   [demanding and angry] Smile!

ZELDA   . . . hoping to see me diminutive and cowering, a tee-hee doll bride. Something in that tone is ominous.

SCOTT   They call it admiration!

ZELDA   I think it is a desire to crush motion. See? [*Zelda points to one of the men in back*] He flexes the muscles of his cheeks [*man flexes the muscles of his cheeks*] He "smiles" (if you can call baring the teeth a smile!)

VOICE   Smile!

ZELDA   I have learned to mirror that look, lips stretched across rows of glistening teeth, eyes obscene with underlying hate. Do I have it? [*Zelda shows her version of man's smile*] SMILE!

Scott laughs

VOICE   SMILE

ZELDA   I shone back at them their glinting tyranny.

VOICE   What a pretty . . .

ZELDA   [*Loudly*] I called them tyrants (You whitewashed, greedy-gutted goons!) . . .

53

Scott laughs again

VOICE [*Whistles*] Whee-whoo!

ZELDA   [*More loudly*] . . . and their tyranny . . . (venereal, hotnutted oligarchs!) . . .

Scott laughs some more

VOICE   [*Oily*] Hi, Gorgeous!

ZELDA   [*More loudly still*] . . . the Tyranny of Smiles!

SCOTT   Oh, she was wonderful! Zelda could handle anything!

ZELDA   Goofo, Goofo, sweetheart, when I am out walking, you are as distant from me as a photograph of a dearly departed loved one. I feel as if I am overlooked by buzzards who have stared at too many photographs of dead horse-flesh to remember why they ever approached a live one to begin with, so caught up in the emblems of their need, they starve! . . . Intimidated by these poor, desperate creatures? Never! [*aside*] Though I could see the winning of my autonomy was going to take some doing!

TYRANNY OF SMILES LEERERS have receded during Zelda's speech, but they remain upstage. Ernest, dressed as before, with gun, enters.

ERNEST   I don't see what they were all running around after *her* for. I remember the day I met her. She didn't look like the great beauty *that* day!

ZELDA   They say I destroyed Scott. Anyone will tell you that. Ernest especially wasn't one of my great admirers.

ERNEST   I knew she was bad for Scott from the beginning.

54

SCOTT   Feelings turned floodtide at the sight of her . . .

ERNEST   He could have been a great writer like *me*, but she ruined him.

SCOTT   She set something off in me . . . an undertow of feeling for her—

ERNEST   In plain language, he was a drowning man.

ZELDA   [*oblivious of Ernest*] Scott appreciated me!

ERNEST   As for Zelda, her "indian eyes," as they liked to call them, were bloodshot. She looked boozed out.

ZELDA   I'll admit I'd been known to take one. [*Zelda sits at table and pours herself a drink of bourbon in a short glass. One for her, one for Scott. Scott leans back in chair*] Scott liked one, too.

GERTRUDE STEIN   Bourbon, Bourbon in shining glasses . . .

ZELDA   I liked whiskey . . .

Zelda & Scott Test the Magic Potions

GERTRUDE STEIN   Bourbon, bourbon broke their asses.

ZELDA   . . . neat—or over—and Scott did, too. [*they drink*] On summer afternoons I liked a cool drink, maybe gin and lime [*Zelda pours gin and tonic in tall glasses for herself and Scott*]. I liked campari with a twist [*pours two more*] — and Scott and I would go . . .

SCOTT   Would go . . .

ZELDA   . . . to the Plaza Hotel . . .

SCOTT   . . . in the afternoons . . .

ZELDA   . . . Yes . . . and drink there [*Zelda puts shaved ice and contents of cocktail shaker into long-stemmed glasses for her and Scott*] . . . green iced daiquiris.

SCOTT   The Plaza knew how to make an iced daiquiri. Sometimes they're too sweet, but these were . . .

ZELDA   . . . Delicious! Sometimes we'd go to the Ritz bar and we'd have . . .

SCOTT   . . . a cognac [*Scott pours two cognacs in small liqueur glasses*].

ZELDA   Yes, I liked that.

SCOTT   We liked that.

ZELDA   We liked that.

They sit back and drink

ZELDA   They have a name for our thirst.

SCOTT   They named it . . .

ZELDA   . . . Alcoholism. Oh, just, you know, a misplaced passion for risk! [*Momentarily subdued, as if remembering something*] I should have stayed home like Nora Joyce and dusted and mopped the floor.

ERNEST   She didn't.

ZELDA   I didn't want to! I should have stayed home like Mrs. Eliot and shot up instead of parading my addictions in public.

SCOTT   Why wasn't she more careful?

ZELDA   I should have been there for you to come home dead drunk to.

ERNEST   Instead they came home dead drunk together.

ZELDA   I'd have never learned what a stupid life a bright man could lead. I'd have thought you were out doing something glamorous!

SCOTT   But Darling, our life *was* glamorous! I was a success!

Spectre of Virginia Woolf enters. The following dialogue moves rapidly.

VIRGINIA   Everyone knows that . . .

ERNEST   Scott was successful.

VIRGINIA   . . . You have been . . .

GERTRUDE STEIN   Success won't save them.

VIRGINIA   . . . in every way all that anyone could be.

SCOTT   They interviewed us.

ZELDA   They sought out Scott.

SCOTT   We were worth a lot of money.

ZELDA   Scott was valuable.

SCOTT   They said we were the two most beautiful people in the world.

ZELDA   I felt eclipsed.

SCOTT   But Zelda, you were brilliant!

ZELDA   I wanted to keep up the pace.

SCOTT   I made her the heroine of all my stories!

ZELDA   I went nearly to death to keep them amused.

SCOTT   That our life together might be putting demands on her she couldn't handle never occurred to me . . .

ZELDA   I burned in thin air while they sat back and clocked it.

SCOTT   After all, she was *Zelda*!

GERTRUDE STEIN   They wanted the deepest extravagance.

SCOTT   Actually, my fantasies of her were better than she was. [*He pours himself a drink*]

ZELDA   Oh, wow! Did you hear *that*?

ERNEST   Scott started to write schlock stories for the *Saturday Evening Post*.

VIRGINIA   I can't read . . .

SCOTT   [*defensively*] I did it for the money!

ERNEST   It was *her* fault!

VIRGINIA   . . . and I can't concentrate . . .

ZELDA   The fox coat didn't fix it.

SCOTT   [*drinking*] How mistaken I was. How was I to have known that the very rich . . .

VIRGINIA   I think I am going mad again.

SCOTT   . . . were different from us. I learned too late that the . . .

GERTRUDE STEIN   Well-to-do

ERNEST   Played out moneybags, brutes and bores

ZELDA   The well-to-do

SCOTT   Do what?

ERNEST   They suck.

ZELDA   . . . are sucks.

GERTRUDE STEIN   They suck and suck.

SCOTT   But the flagstone porches! The shining Pierce Arrow automobiles! . . .

ERNEST   Everyone wanting to buy his way into humanity . . . Pull!

ZELDA   . . . and no one willing to pay the price [*blast*]

SCOTT   All the smiling gardens . . .

ERNEST   . . . mask a brutality . . . [*Tyranny of Smiles Leerers step forward*]

SCOTT   All the trailing fuchsia blooms . . .

ERNEST   . . . could not hide. . .   Pull! [*Tyranny of Smiles Leerers advance another step*]

GERTRUDE STEIN   Could not hide [*blast*]

ZELDA   . . . could neither mask nor hide

SCOTT   . . . neither mask . . .

ERNEST   . . . nor hide . . .

ZELDA   . . . the underlying brutality [*Tyranny of Smiles Leerers advance another step*]

ERNEST Pull!

SCOTT [*Shaken*] The greed! [*blast*] [*Tyranny of Smiles Leerers take another step closely behind Ernest, Scott and Zelda*]

ZELDA He began to recognize . . .

SCOTT I began to see . . .

ZELDA That the very rich . . .

ERNEST That the very rich . . .

ZELDA Were different from us . . .

SCOTT Were altogether different from us.

ZELDA We bought . . .

ERNEST They bought . . .

SCOTT We bought . . .

GERTRUDE STEIN They bought . . .

GERTRUDE STEIN, ERNEST, SCOTT and ZELDA The wrong dream!

ZELDA It was not as easily bought as we'd thought.

SCOTT It was expensive.

ERNEST Sure rapids! White water! Guts Ball!

Exit Ernest. Tyranny of Smiles Leerers move back behind veils.

SCOTT   Love, Freedom, Success . . .

ZELDA   All the great prizes to be wrested from life

SCOTT   Everything we'd wanted . . .

ZELDA   [*longingly*] We'd wanted

SCOTT   . . . turned out to be a disappointment

GERTRUDE STEIN   Alas, there is always a fly in the ointment

ZELDA   [*sadly*] In this world, nothing is perfect. [*Then laughing*] Well, isn't that just too god damned bad?!

Gentle People, sitting back in your chairs, never moved by failure, never knowing what it is to try something that might be beyond the scope of your powers, don't be too quick to think you've avoided [*conspiratorially*] them [*pointing at the Tyranny of Smiles Leerers*] SPLAT against the parameters of Desire. Who are they lurking there? Inhuman brutes? Oh, no! They're shades condemned to the netherworld of risk. They've no masks to prettify their woes. Do you fear them? Rightly so. Their domain is an underworld of dreams and they want to draw you in! [*Tyranny of Smiles Leerers beckon in a sinister manner*] Show some grit! Though a bird in flight might break its wing against a glass or wheel into a wall, the false protection of a cage is surer damage, I know it! Air! Air! The Promise of Air!

SCOTT   [*steps forward and makes an announcement*]

"Zelda's Dream
The Legacy of Excess"

Lights blacken on all but Zelda and the Tyranny of Smiles Leerers as Zelda relates her dream. The dialogue marked VOICE is, as before, divided among the Leerers.

ZELDA One late November day, creeping winter darkening the sky, a rain began to fall while Scott and I were out walking in a strange part of town. We took refuge in a nightclub where we drank a lovely fluid from amber glasses. Perhaps we were drugged. I overheard a man at the next table recount a story of an impotent man who bought a hangman's noose . . . supposed to give him an erection, then unhang him . . . But the trick noose knotted and he jacked off eternally . . . as if passion were a gimmick or a reflex action. The tale struck a chord of familiarity with me I did not like. I wanted out! When Scott wasn't looking, I slipped through the door into the wide city. On My Own!

I moved past pigeons and men in grey hats. A stiff-skirted mother on the chair of a church smoothed her son's wet hair. I felt protected by the clichés of quiet lives. A swallow dived in the sky . . . Where was I?

VOICE [*like a town cryer*] Nine-teen twen-ty one and all is we-ll!

ZELDA [*mysteriously*] I held the map upside down and moved deeper into mirrored blocks. Rainy day changed to rainy night, darkness, the sky filling with it. Deeper down I went, feeling freer—streets filling with . . . what was it? Night lights began—night taking over everywhere. *I wanted something too alive to have a name!*

My desire conjured ruined souls, and as figures in an allegory teach, these casualties of life warned me! The first to appear seemed harmless enough [*while Zelda continues this sequence, the Tyranny of Smiles Leerers approach her one by one*] . . . a newsman slumped on the wheel of his truck. Just a man asleep on the job. Why did I feel alarmed?

Next, in an alley named Adler, I saw a drunk . . .

Zelda's Day of Reckoning in the Province of Desire: The Consequence of a Dream

VOICE   Whatsa matter, hon-ey?

ZELDA   He looked out of control!

VOICE   They were wanting.

VOICE   Gimme quatah, come on ba-abe.

ZELDA   A one-armed man in a cape rolled up my sleeves looking for marks . . .

VOICE   Hey, Sister, Hey!

ZELDA   What would I know about grey-faced women and never healing sores? I passed a dead mouse torn apart by a cat, passed stains on the sidewalk sunk deeper than islands of snot could ever sink. Behind the wall of a building rose a gargling howl!

VOICE   Zelda!

ZELDA   Two men stood in the doorway of an abandoned hotel. The flabby one vomited hamburger gruel . . .

VOICE   Zelda Sayre!

ZELDA   Pus poured from a hole in one's head right above his ear! They called to me . . .

VOICE   Zelda, Zelda Sayre!

ZELDA   All the junkies knew my name!

GERTRUDE STEIN Too far, Too far
She was going too far!

ZELDA The safety tripped, the bottom dropped. A hell of being ringed me round . . . A desperation born of risk! Affinity! . . . A dare!

I felt a curious spinning and vertigo of motion as if I were flying into an abyss . . . along with it the peculiar joy one feels at the precipice of a great height (The sailors call it 'Raptures of the Deep') a desire to dive into gravity!

At the end limit of risk I knew: *What was wanted was something beautiful*! To see the sky again backcombed by morning, the blackest midnight baffled by stars!

I whirled around to stop the plunge and faced a darkened storefront streaked by rain. There across it, her long hair streaming, her pockets weighted by stones . . .

Spectre of Virginia Woolf appears in window/mirror

"Virginia! [*Zelda calls to reflection*] Image trapped in a final frame of defeat! I, too, could cry and sink, waving goodbye forever at the meridian of sanity. I, too, am afraid of these wanged-out arenas of feeling. The world can seem a perilous place. Yet I would pull you up again from your dark bed in the River Ouse. Haunt me no more! Come up in full heat, raw and shaking! For once, Virginia, undrown! [*Zelda stops a moment. Image of Virginia is dispelled from glass*]

Did she? No, not even in a dream.

What has passed has passed they say, they say . . .

GERTRUDE STEIN [*spells*] F - A - C - T.

ZELDA . . . and what is done is done . . .

GERTRUDE STEIN The die is cast, perhaps.

ZELDA ... Yet for a dead being she affected me greatly and for a dead deed her suicide trouble me still.

GERTRUDE STEIN F - A - C - T.

ZELDA Relentlessly the energy of each life travels the universe of blood, transforming ordinary order. Virginia disappeared. (Was I nuts?) and I was shocked to find myself back in the neighborhood of the club I had left. Again I heard the happy "Hi"s ...

VOICE [*friendly now*] Hi!

VOICE Hello there!

ZELDA ... and "How-dee-doo"s of good folk and smiling streets

VOICE Hey, there!

ZELDA (Was it mask or parallel fact?) ... Everything seemed ... O-O-kay!

I entered the door through which I'd come. [*Tempo builds*] The place was crowded ... my damp clothes began steaming in the heat. I could feel the heat of bodies leaning into one another, and you, dear, [*meaning Scott and drawing him back into the action*] foreign and familiar at the same time. I was HOT! All the while a wandering horn backboned by drums [*Zelda's music begins*] slipped a needle of sound beneath my skin. Though my vision wanted a sunstruck room with ranunculas in a vase and clouds of baby's breath, I knew I could move here as well as anywhere. I stood, then turned and turned.

The music is lyrical, nostalgic jazz. As Zelda dances, the Tyranny of Smiles Leerers back off and disappear. Ernest enters.

65

ERNEST   She'll ruin you, Scott.

Music ends. Zelda stops dancing.

ZELDA   When the music stopped, I looked around to see, the saxophone player's lip had split. I awakened.

ERNEST   She'll ruin you, man.

ZELDA   Now, what do you make of that?

SCOTT   The drivespring of the personality is taut.

ZELDA   The motion of its letting go is relentless.

SCOTT   I watched you go on with who you were and knew there was no stopping you.

ERNEST   When it's all over you and Scott will be nothing more than two lists of symptoms in a doctor's notepad.

SCOTT   [*dazed*] Silver strands of water fractured by birds . . .

Zelda
Doesn't Know

ZELDA   I don't know . . . I don't know . . . but something nameless, slowly moving, nearly unnoticeable can easily take hold. It blunts. It deadens. It anesthetizes eyes . . . Can I explain?

ERNEST   She's crazy.

ZELDA   Somewhere is lost in the shrinking fields of the republic, a passion, a care, and nobody's certain that anything is wrong at all!

GERTRUDE STEIN   If it had a face
                If you could name it

ZELDA   I must do something!

ERNEST   You're a loser and you'll make a loser out of Scott!
  [*He picks up his gun and runs offstage*]

Curtain. End Part II

PART III

PART III

Same stage arrangement. Gertrude in her customary position. Table with one chair. Writing paper, fountain pen. Under table are bouquet of roses, basket of strawberries, bottle of champagne with glass and a wide-brimmed sunhat covered with flowers. Behind veils are easels and canvases, palettes and brushes on floor. Stage left is a ballet bar where Zelda, in white leotard dress, is doing ballet exercises. To stage right is a mirror. Scott, Ernest and Virginia Woolf are present.

ZELDA   [*with dreamlike intensity*] Now I'll call it more than it was. I did and I will! "Everything is more than it is!" . . . They took my temperature for *that*!

SCOTT   She was hot!

ZELDA   98.6 and that was the fact.

GERTRUDE STEIN   F - A - C - T

ZELDA   They told me life was ordinary. I didn't believe them
They wanted to see an immense woman stand up in
    her shoes and sing
They wanted a poet (I am not afraid to say it!)
They wanted a soul

GERTRUDE STEIN   She tried.

*Zelda Knocks
Herself Out:
A Long Process*

ZELDA   I tried.

GERTRUDE STEIN   She tried and tried.

ZELDA   We all tried. Ernest wrote it down on his pad. [*Zelda picks up paper*] See? [*points to it*] That's it! Right there.

ERNEST   The square root of desire.

ZELDA   I saw him compute it.

SCOTT   Oh, what a machine, this desire . . .

ZELDA   This greed!

ERNEST   Technology of passion.

ZELDA   Each cog locks with every other cog.

SCOTT   Chug-a-chug.

ERNEST   Ugh-chug-a-chug.

ZELDA   Every . . .

GERTRUDE STEIN   Each piece . . .

ZELDA   . . . piece interchangeable with every other.

GERTRUDE STEIN   Each piece . . .

SCOTT   Chug-a-ugh-a.

ERNEST   Chug-a-boom.

ZELDA   I was a part of it all . . .

GERTRUDE STEIN   A piece of the puzzle.

ZELDA   A piece of the puzzle only!
   [*Zelda sits at table, writes, gets up and reads:*]
      "Climbing green vine slipped beautifully around another
      vine . . . Wisteria cornucopia-ing wallsides . . . corn-
      flowers stud stairway . . . Verticals of venetian blind
      breaks yellow bands across tile floor . . . Bougain-
      villea . . ."

[*Zelda looks up and says:*] Look at that word! Wouldn't you want to say it whether you could pronounce it or not? . . . Bougainvillea!" [*resumes*]
   "Birds . . . White sky
   Black tulips and ragged robins!"

O Goofo, so taken into the world, us so warm in its heart!
   "Laughter smoothes the brow
   Easy hand on smoothed face
   The heart spills its lap of daffodils and iris . . ."

[*Zelda whispers:*] Desire!

ERNEST   But the writing didn't go well at all.

SCOTT   In fact, I had to sign my name to her stories to get them published.

ERNEST   Scott drew on her diaries for his novels . . . yet we all knew she was a second-rate writer.

SCOTT   *Third* rate!

ZELDA   All right, then, *third* rate. [*exercising at the ballet bar*] Why did I enjoy life? What did I want to write for? when everyone knew . . .

GERTRUDE STEIN   They knew.

SCOTT   We all knew.

ZELDA   They knew I was going to fail. What was my problem? Why didn't I stop? I'll tell you why. I loved to write! [*Zelda continues to exercise at the ballet bar*] If I had knuckled down and done something, anything at all . . .

SCOTT   She had no discipline.

ZELDA   . . . the clichés would never have shown their cracks. We would have lived . . .

73

SCOTT   We could have lived . . .

GERTRUDE STEIN   They might have lived . . .

ZELDA and SCOTT   . . . Happily Ever After . . .

ZELDA   Maybe.

SCOTT   Maybe.

GERTRUDE STEIN   Maybe.

ZELDA   [*sits at table and writes and reads:*]
"Left alone! A place to be!
Protected by an arc of nodding heads . . ."

SCOTT   Why did she have to write?

ERNEST   She wanted to do you in.

ZELDA   [*wads up paper, writes and reads:*] "A small bird . . .
with black eye . . . and white throat . . ." [*She wads it up*]

SCOTT   Why did she have to do it?

ZELDA   I lived a lyric masquerade when everywhere brute
words fell. The live lyric was an upper lip silvered by snot,
as real (*their* word) as ever a "brilliant eye." On every street
unsounded feeling fell. Possibilities! Shit! I swore to be
true!

For one lyric, take your ordered world of tape-recorded
holidays, good-mornings and polite toast!

The cluckers tsk-tsk to me . . .

VOICE   Beware, beware! Gravity ends free fall!
Beware, beware of gravity!

ZELDA   . . . they say. [*Zelda goes to table and writes, reads,
gets up, sits down:*] "I float . . . clouds move across build-
ings . . . birds ring the park . . . a breeze gentled by rain at
the back moves uphill . . . A rush of clouds buries me back-
wards . . . grey sky, Paris maybe, in the rain . . .

Pull the cord! I land late and maybe *never!*"

VOICE   Beware, beware of gravity!

ZELDA   I wrote it down it seemed tentative . . . Now language certain and final, the fright and floundering of getting it down . . . always inadequate, these shabby replicas
of feeling. Pretty putrid and absolute and terminal as
death, this putting life down on the page, trying to make it
"come out" and it doesn't except as some different final,
created event . . . using the agreed-upon sounds of the
larger society of which I am a part [*Zelda tears up her
writing*]

SCOTT   A piece.

GERTRUDE STEIN   A piece of the puzzle only.

ZELDA   [*chanting now*] I pay credit to the confusion that
will not adhere to the agreed-upon sound. My chaos never
carried through that medium. Language does not do nor
even any sound at all . . . These searing transformations,
unexpressed . . . soundless and without air . . .
Though all the words were at my disposal they would not
hold heat! O bullshit language. O bullshit past.

I knew if I could once sit down and talk like myself everything would be "O—K"! So . . . . . . "unhuh" and "what?"
and "yeah?" and "how come it's" "why?" [*pause*] I sounded
silly.

ERNEST   Yes, she did.

SCOTT   I'm afraid she did.

ZELDA   Sometimes I've felt I'm in that vacuum Ernest's always wanting, screaming in tongues.

SCOTT   I didn't always understand her.

ZELDA   I've often felt that I'm on some moon . . .

ERNEST   She could be distant . . .

ZELDA   . . . endlessly outside the intimacy of ordinary life . . .

ERNEST   She was strange.

ZELDA   They said I was too intense . . .

ERNEST   She bored into me with her hawk's eyes.

SCOTT   I felt myself pulled in.

ZELDA   . . . or not there at all. I thought I had given over totally . . .

ERNEST   I couldn't understand her.

ZELDA   . . . but they told me I was holding back . . . [pause] What is it people share with one another?

SCOTT   I tried to reach her.

ZELDA   There's an intimacy people speak of I'm afraid I've never known . .

VIRGINIA   I feel certain . . .

ZELDA   Some place in the psyche no one has touched . . .

VIRGINIA   . . . I am going mad again.

ZELDA   [*afraid*] Oh, Goofo! Did we know each other?

SCOTT   Was it love?

ZELDA   Would calling it that suddenly make our lives together . . .

VIRGINIA   . . . without me you could work . . .

ZELDA   . . . beautiful?

SCOTT   Love.

ZELDA   Love . . . Is that what it was?

SCOTT   I love you.

ZELDA   I love you.

ERNEST   [*stepping forward and changing the mood:*] She didn't look like the great beauty *that* day! She looked like hell! "Scott," I said to him [*Ernest addresses dialogue in quotation marks to Scott*] and him not looking too good either, "She'll ruin you, Scott."

SCOTT   I heard you the last time.

ERNEST   She's destroying you, man.

ZELDA   [*exercising*] I hated to admit it then, but I can now . . . Ernest was right. I needed too much help to do one thing for Scott. [*to Scott:*] Goofo, I who wanted so much freedom for myself, forgot to let you breathe . . . I who wanted so much love, forgot to love you. I am sorry, dear, love. Forgive me.

SCOTT   I was in no better shape than she was. We were kill-
ing each other slowly.

ZELDA   I needed something of my own!

*Zelda goes over to easel, stands back to look at painting. In the
background are sounds of laughter. A group of from 3-5 men
examine the paintings and laugh. They are the VOICE in the
following. Dialogue divided among them. They speak like
newscasters.*

ZELDA   [*to audience*] What are they laughing at over there,
you ask? That's an exhibit . . . Those are my paintings.

VOICE   Grotesque!

VOICE   Disfigured!

VOICE   *"Last week . . . Zelda Fitzgerald showed her pictures
. . . She was hoping they would gratify her great ambition—
to earn her own living.*

ZELDA   On the cover of the exhibit they had printed:

VOICE   *"Sometimes madness is wisdom"*

ZELDA   Jesus Christ, did they have to say *that*?
[*pause. Laughter dies down*] Why did I keep on painting?
Well, I'll tell you. Painting pushed my spirit. I liked the
feeling. I loved to paint! [*laughter starts again*] . . . and
what are they laughing at over there? That's my play,
Scandalabra. Oh, yes. I stuck my neck out on that one,
too. I was a dilettante at everything except compulsion.

VOICE   *"There is probably nothing more embarrassing to
any normally intelligent observer in the theater than to*

78

witness a fantasy that has gone haywire . . . But 'gone haywire' is surely the only way of describing the progress, in a prologue and two acts of Mrs. Fitzgerald's play."

ZELDA   [*thinking about it*] The play was the least of it! Yet I will tell you, the theatre *was* exhilarating, and I have to admit . . . I loved it!

[*Zelda dances some more*]

I also liked to dance. I threw myself into ballet. At twenty-eight. Too old, you say? Well, I *was* too old. I knew it, Scott knew it, [*Zelda gestures to Gertrude Stein*] my teacher, the great Madame Egorova, knew it, but I did it anyway . . .

SCOTT   Why did she do it?

ZELDA   . . . because I liked it . . . even though we knew I would always be second rate . . .

SCOTT   *Third* rate!

ZELDA   All *right*! *Third* rate! [*Zelda changes pace*] I took as my model, Madame Egorova. [*Zelda gestures to Gertrude Stein, who will play the voice of Mme. Egorova. Gertrude will change her accent so audience will get the idea*] Here was a woman who stood on her own. Through discipline and endurance, she had shaped her own life.

Egorova was good to me! She said:

Madame Egorova

GS as MME EGOROVA   Though you started late, if you work hard . . .

ZELDA   Though I started late, if I worked hard . . .

SCOTT   Though she started late, if she worked hard . . .

GS as MME EGOROVA   You might be . . .

ZELDA   I might aspire to become . . .

GS as MME EGOROVA   . . . a member of . . .

ZELDA   . . . me, a part . . .

GS as MME EGOROVA   . . . of the San Carlos Company
corps de ballet . . .

SCOTT   Impossible!

GS as MME EGOROVA   . . . Naples . . .

ERNEST   She's lousy!

ZELDA   She said I might be . . .

GS as MME EGOROVA   . . . part of a company.

ZELDA   Me? Gee! a part . . .

GS as MME EGOROVA   . . . a piece of a company.

SCOTT   I couldn't believe it!

ZELDA   I wanted something of my own.

GS as MME EGOROVA   . . . and you shall have it!

ERNEST   No!

ZELDA   Egorova!

SCOTT   No!

ZELDA   One evening I brought her an armload of roses [*Zelda goes to table, gets roses and basket of strawberries, champagne and long-stemmed glass*] and laid them at her feet [*Zelda lays roses at Gertrude Stein's feet*]. I brought her a basket of strawberries [*Zelda uncorks champagne, pours out a glass*] and floated three of them for her in a glass of champagne [*Zelda puts strawberries in the glass and hands to Gertrude Stein*]

I loved her to embarrassment.

GERTRUDE STEIN   Embarrassment.

ERNEST   Zelda was an embarrassment.

ZELDA   I worked.

GERTRUDE STEIN   She worked.

ZELDA   . . . and was a good student.

GERTRUDE STEIN   She worked and worked.

ZELDA   I worked at my dancing even though I knew I'd never be the best . . .

GERTRUDE STEIN   She worked and worked and worked.

SCOTT   Why? I couldn't understand.

GERTRUDE STEIN   She worked.

ZELDA   . . . because I loved it!

GERTRUDE STEIN   She loved to work.

ZELDA   I liked to raise my leg like this and then extend my arm [*Zelda raises leg and extends arm*] I liked to bend [*she*

81

bends] and rise again like this [*she rises*]. I liked to stand up on one toe [*she stands up on one toe*] and feel my limbs rise free! I liked to turn and spin and spin [*she spins*] This was liberty!

SCOTT   Why did she want to dance when she had such a wonderful life with me? I didn't like her dancing at all.

ERNEST   She was ungainly.

ZELDA   I loved to move!

SCOTT   Stop her!

ERNEST   Stop.

ZELDA   They wanted to stop me.

ERNEST   You'll fail.

SCOTT   You'll fail.

ZELDA   To thrust my hand inside a flame and come away with its blue white heat? I was ordinary all right . . . with a passion. [*Zelda whispers*] Desire!

SCOTT   I had to admit it, she was game.

Zelda dances again

SCOTT   I had no one to do things with.

VIRGINIA   I know that I am spoiling your life . . .

ERNEST   One day she changed into her ballet costume in a cab! The thing of it was: She was really a shitty dancer.

SCOTT   Yet she turned circles, odd her way with it [*Zelda turns*]

82

ERNEST [*watching Zelda dance*] Yes, odd, the way she turned.

SCOTT The room transfixed to check her balance.

VIRGINIA If anyone could have saved me, it would have been you.

Ernest and Scott move back

ZELDA I worked as never before . . . morning to night . . . I worked at the bar: pirouette, plié, arabesque [*Zelda executes these steps*] I pushed and pushed . . .

SCOTT Something in the way she did it . . .

ERNEST . . . made the blood run cold.

ZELDA . . . and some damage was being done, like a bruise you don't notice. [*Zelda speeds up her dancing*] Faster and faster I worked. Eyes tight shut [*Zelda clinches her eyes shut*] white inside, yellow [*Zelda opens eyes*] I opened my eyes, heaving breath and there it was at the periphery of vision: a touch of red. I blinked [*Zelda blinks*] and looked straight at it: Gone! Aha! . . . I began again, dancing . . . tour jeté, plié [*Zelda dances*] arabesque — push . . . eyes tight [*Zelda closes eyes*] tissue of sweat . . . push . . . eyes open. [*Zelda opens eyes*] The ballet studio began to vibrate — the yellows stood out and then the oranges — the wood of the table began to glow — the edge of the bookcase moved out beside itself! A real orange hurtled from a real bowl! More and more vivid the colors became until RED, a red aura rose around the shelf, a red-orange disc rose above the lamp, the red shade pulsed beside itself, doubled in intensity and leapt from its ordinary place — even the air took on the red vibrating waves!

*Zelda
Sees Red*

83

Dancers by Zelda Fitzgerald

My body sweat like a bleeding window—a wall of red waved from the floor washing at my eyes—blood pulse!

I was afraid of myself.

Zelda
Flips Out

Oh God. Stop it! Stop it!

I clenched my eyes tight . . . opened again to the white ceiling that trailed amoebic snails and silverfish . . . thank God . . . white at last . . . and crystalline . . . but when I looked down again, the air was BEATING!

VIRGINIA I feel certain . . .

ZELDA My insides were out at last.

VIRGINIA . . . I am going mad again.

VOICE 10 milligrams.

SCOTT Our life together is my material.

ZELDA Put me out.

Zelda in
Retrograde

SCOTT None of it is your material.

VOICE 15 milligrams.

SCOTT Second rate.

ZELDA Morphine.

SCOTT Third rate.

VOICE 10 milligrams.

VIRGINIA . . . and I shan't recover this time.

ZELDA [*speech is slow and slurred*] Soundless turning . . .
black again . . . different versions of density . . . slanting,

turning . . . not a perfect circle at all . . . None of it was perfect . . . None of it . . .

Where are we?

"even you now all bones . . ."

they want me drown down . . . all right, too . . . I hope it was . . . falling down . . . love . . . I have a need to give it . . .

Long pause as Zelda sleeps. Her music plays. When it stops, she begins to talk as if she were observing herself.

ZELDA   I wasn't really crazy . . . I had just slipped into high gear. When I awakened, all the colors were back in their proper places.

VIRGINIA   I can't fight any longer.

ZELDA   No escape now.

ERNEST   They had her.

SCOTT   The ordinary.

ZELDA   White walls in white rooms.

GERTRUDE STEIN   Freud's in his heaven
and all's right with the world

ERNEST   Plain geometry.

ZELDA   Everywhere the grid.

SCOTT   Dr. Thomas Rennes, Valmont . . . the hospital at Malmaison . . . Les Rives de Prangins asylum on the shores of Lake Geneva.

ZELDA   That was Europe.

ERNEST   They hit all the nuthouses.

SCOTT   Then the U.S. . . .

ZELDA   . . . and more "hospitals" . . .

SCOTT   Phipps . . . Craig House . . . Sheppard Pratt . . . Dr. Forel and Dr. Mildred Squires. From here on out, everything we did was a euphemism.

ERNEST   How *is* Zelda?

ZELDA   They would ask . . .

VOICE   How *is* she?

ZELDA   Yes. It seemed such a right thing to say . . . "Zelda is mad." Everyone agreed. And *perfectly* mad at that! How well it suited me!

VOICE   How *is* Zelda?

VOICE   How is Zelda today?

ZELDA   Everyone was in a big hurry to have me put out of the way.

GERTRUDE STEIN   Drivespring of the spirit
In a man's breast
In a woman's breast

SCOTT   They named her personal vision 'insanity.'

ZELDA   When all I'd wanted to do was to transform life with a beautiful act. They called me a schiz.

SCOTT   . . . but real life is lived beyond all their names.

GERTRUDE STEIN   Certainly life is lived beyond all their names.

ERNEST   All their names! [*Ernest exits*]

ZELDA   And worst of all, I was burning out. [*to Scott:*] Sometimes I see the coolest part of me reflected in your face . . .

SCOTT   . . . as remote as an ocean bottom. What can be the vast barrenness of your presence . . .

ZELDA   . . . shadows on the show.

SCOTT   I want the amber eye of life!

ZELDA   Seemed as if some great event would save us . . . but I had stopped living inside my eyes.

SCOTT   Slowly the lines travelled her hands.

ZELDA   They looked like chicken's feet!

SCOTT   None of the major alterations for which we had prepared ever happened. My golden girl!

ZELDA   Leaves circle the stairwell
The dial of the radio drifts
Cockroaches have eaten the sound

Scott left me in the South. This was his last letter.

Scott goes behind the veils and delivers his letter

SCOTT [*reads:*]
"Garden of Allah Hotel
Hollywood, California

Dear Zelda,
Cement blocks carry remembrances of bodies: this one's
hands, that one's legs, Barrymore's profile deep-sixed forever! Hollywood Boulevard! Tessellated pink stars, gold
banded, the notable's name in gold and an emblem of the
area of his achievement; the camera, the microphone, in a
golden circle beneath his name." Immortality.

SCOTT [*stops reading and calls out:*] Zelda, can you hear
[*resumes:*] "It's lovely here" [*he looks up*] but something's
wrong.

[*Scott continues:*] "I mean seductive. Fleshy flowers, neat
lawns, pomegranate highways! Everything is flesh, seed,
sun! I am as tranquil as a mogul!" Beauty.

[*Aside:*] There are three different kinds of hair and a cigarette butt in the sink. The ventilator clicks. The toilet is
unflushed. The bathroom at Hollywood and Vine!.

ZELDA I wanted to tell him something . . .

SCOTT Zelda!

ZELDA . . . but he couldn't hear me anymore.

SCOTT Where am I? Marooned on a junkpile of myth!

ZELDA He wrote to Scottie:

SCOTT [*reads:*]
"Dearest Scottie,
And Little Shirley Temple will be your very best friend.
And Little Freddie Bartholomew and little all the rest of
them . . ."

89

[*Scott looks up:*] Jesus! What is it coming to? [*resumes:*] "Quietly now the sprinklers' hush. Steadily the maids make their way among Spanish tiles."

Almost like a hospital or . . . [*in fear:*] Zelda, exiled to the asylum of the provinces, what was it we wanted? Sun? an aqua pool? the cry of an ugly bird? Total wonder!

ZELDA   Perhaps we were bound to be disappointed.

SCOTT   We are baggy-eyed gangsters staring at empty safes. I look in the mirror and know that I wrote it already: Poor Son of a Bitch. Hollywood looks so much like what happened to us. [*Scott exits*]

ZELDA   Then they wrote me Scott had died. Love, don't leave me! Oh, Goofo, I reach into the fields of death to pull you out. You're gone! The last person who knew who I was.

VIRGINIA   You have been in every way all that anyone could be.

Zelda goes to table, picks up a big hat with flowers on it and puts it on

ZELDA   I went to meet my childhood friend, Lucy. I waited for her in the garden. She came and didn't recognize me.

"Lucy, I am Zelda Sayre," I called to her. She ran away! Am I so changed?

[*Zelda removes hat. As if to Scott:*] I visit Scottie once in a while. She just had another child, but dear, you know, I was never a family person. I am here in the asylum which is no asylum, talked to by authorities. What do they know? [*Sighs*] No one remembers us at all.

[*Pause, changes tone and says to audience:*] Have I come this whole way to advise you to stay home? Oh no! oh, no! [*Zelda yells:*] Lucy! I am Zelda Sayre!

GERTRUDE STEIN AS ZELDA'S MOTHER [*Using southern accent as Zelda's mother:*] Zelda, Zelda honey, you spent too much time on the roof, honey. Come down, now. Aren't you tired, honey? Please come down.

ZELDA I ain't tired, Mama, no I ain't . . . but it appears, Mama, it does appear . . . we do have a conflagration here. It's hot! and though I am dreaming I do feel heat. The heat is dreadful. It's so hot up here. The heat is rising from a thousand places, Mama. What is it? I have felt it before. It is hotter than summer in Montgomery ever was, Mama, Hotter than I ever thought it would be. Mama! I am alive up here. Who is here with me? Smoke and this heat! I am on fire!

Scott in the grave, I dream, I burn!

GERTRUDE STEIN AS ZELDA'S MOTHER Zelda, dear, why are you always up there? We are waiting for you to come down. Who are you? And which one today?

ZELDA [*quoting herself:*]
"The air shines and it is yellow and white at the same time
This is the gift air and the day holding round it
I want (I wanted) to blow into life a brilliance
as into a flame to fan it
I want (I wanted) *you know*, everything!"

[*To Scott:*] I wanted to be that for you, Scott . . . the exquisite, moving creature. I wanted to be long-necked and extravagant—darling . . .

VIRGINIA I don't think two people could have been . . .

ZELDA . . . the two of us blown up on some cloud like dancers, Scott, dear . . .

VIRGINIA . . . happier than we have been.

ZELDA   . . . their muscles tearing, dull bruise left at the point of elevation.

Zelda dances for a moment. She stops as Gertrude Stein says:

GERTRUDE STEIN as ZELDA'S MOTHER   Scott is dead dear.

ZELDA   [*Holds herself as if suddenly cold*] Sea anemones hug themselves. Even night is exhausted. Stars sleep . . . or is it weep? Cold ocean. Cold sky.

I see never-nodding stars, unceasing infernos of motion. Yes, I would like to say "Stars sleep" but there is no rest. I am *alive* and on *fire*!

VIRGINIA   I can't fight any longer.

ZELDA   [*looks in mirror to see reflection of Virginia Woolf*] You? [*In horror of recognition*] You!

VIRGINIA   So I am doing what seems the best thing to do.

ZELDA   No! Image in a glass, Image only! You shall not weight *me* in water! With this stone I do break! [*Zelda smashes glass and turns to audience*]

Mad? No. Never wasn't. I am *burning*! [*Broken mirror begins to bleed*] Here! A match I throw *out* to you, not *at*! I cut it loose and throw it wide! Catch my heat or call me crazy! I failed for everybody, though that was certainly never my intention. [*Pause*] The cramped gesture opens . . . [*Zelda opens her arms*]

Zelda
Yields
her
Consciousness

GERTRUDE STEIN AS ZELDA'S MOTHER   Zelda . . .

ZELDA   You who called me crippled . . .

GERTRUDE STEIN AS ZELDA'S MOTHER   Zelda . . .

ZELDA   I am the wing!

GERTRUDE STEIN AS ZELDA'S MOTHER   . . . my good
   girl.

Zelda dies.

No Curtain. End Part III

EPILOGUE

Enter Virginia Woolf, carrying a newspaper. She reads:

VIRGINIA   Item: March 10, 1948
"At midnight . . . a fire broke out in the diet kitchen of the
main building where Zelda (Fitzgerald) was sleeping. The
flames shot up a small dumbwaiter shaft to the roof and
leaped out onto each of the floors. The stairways and corri-
dors were filled with smoke . . . There was no automatic
fire-alarm system in the old stone and frame building and
no sprinkler system. The fire escapes were external, but
they were made of wood and quickly caught fire. Firemen
and staff members struggled valiantly to bring the patients
to safety, but they were hampered by locked doors, and by
heavy windows shackled with chains. Nine women were
killed, six of them trapped on the top floor. Zelda (Fitzgerald) died with them."

[*Looks up from paper*] A star drops in the sky, blinds us,
then fails. [*Looks around*]

*Gertrude Stein gets down from her pedestal, moving for the
first time. She kneels over Zelda, lays her head on her stomach
for a moment, then picks her up and carries her offstage. Exit
Gertrude Stein.*

VIRGINIA   Relentlessly spirit travels the universe of blood
transforming ordinary order . . . transforming maybe even
the past. Zelda . . . an offering.

[*Removes from her pockets two large marble ovals and
places them centerstage*] I am really quite late.

*Kneels in front of them. Lights dim until single light shines on
stones. Exit Virginia Woolf.*

Curtain

APPENDIX

Production Note for dance sequences, Parts I and II

If the person playing Zelda feels these dancing sequences are too difficult to manage with the dialogue, then the Director may choose to have a dancer, resembling Zelda and dressed like her, perform them at the appropriate times like a Zelda-spirit. Both women would be on stage at the same time, "Real-Zelda" front center stage; "spirit-Zelda" dancing behind the veils. This device could work well to play off the conflicting strains in Zelda's character, her lyricism versus her raw energy.

Virginia Woolf's suicide note:

"Dearest:
    I feel certain I am going mad again. I feel we can't go through another of those terrible times. And I shan't recover this time. I begin to hear voices, and I can't concentrate. So I am doing what seems the best thing to do. You have been in every way all that anyone could be. I don't think two people could have been happier till this terrible disease came. I can't fight any longer. I know that I am spoiling your life, that without me you could work. And you will I know. You see I can't even write this properly. I can't read. What I want to say is I owe all the happiness of my life to you. You have been entirely patient with me and incredibly good. I want to say that—everybody knows it. If anybody could have saved me it would have been you. Everything has gone from me but the certainty of your goodness. I can't go on spoiling your life any longer.
    I don't think two people could have been happier than we have been.

V."

(from *Virginia Woolf, A Biography* by Quentin Bell, Harcourt Brace Jovanovich, 1972.)